THE 5 STEPS TO HOLISTIC WEALTH

FOR REAL ESTATE INVESTORS

ISBN: 979-8-5855282-6-2

Printed in the United States of America

The 5 Steps to Holistic Wealth *for* Real Estate Investors

TIM S. DAVIS

CONTENTS

DEDICATION

I WOULD LIKE TO DEDICATE THIS BOOK to the many mentors who have helped me. Larry Dobbs who started a little car magazine called Mustang Monthly in Lakeland Florida later went on to be my Sunday School teacher. He introduced me to the concept of building a mastermind of people who could be your team of advisors. He helped me create that team and guided me through the early years of business.

Ted West who introduced me to creative financing in the world of real estate investing. Ted was a great teacher and would talk to me like a son. His words of wisdom gave me insight to what was possible with a little creativity.

Larry Maxwell who sat with me on several occasions to tell me how he built his massive real estate empire. He showed me what was possible and also was an example of what good things could be done in your own community with the wealth that you could accumulate from the vehicle of real estate.

Augie Byllott who mentored me after the bankruptcy and through the rebuilding of my life and businesses. Augie built on all the other things that I had learned before and took me to the next level. His brilliance in creative financing and the example he set in giving back to the community and the world has truly been an inspiration to me.

INTRODUCTION

IF YOU ARE A REAL ESTATE investor who wants to experience holistic wealth and become generous, this book is for you. **Imagine yourself...**

- Experiencing total peace, full of energy, having joyful relationships, running a profitable business, and contributing to a vibrant community.

- Becoming generous with your time and money.

Right now, you might be wondering if it is possible to experience holistic wealth and become generous with your time and money.

Doubting yourself is normal. I used to doubt myself too especially after I went through a divorce, declared bankruptcy, experienced burnout, was 50 lbs. overweight and almost committed suicide.

I overcame my self-doubt when I discovered that I was blocking myself from experiencing holistic wealth and decided to get out of my own way.

In this book, I will help you to overcome any self-doubt so you can experience holistic wealth and become the generous investor everyone loves.

W HEN YOU HEAR THE WORD "WEALTH," what's
the first thing that comes to mind? For many, it is
money, a big house, the hot car, the yacht. Maybe for you it
is exotic vacations. Imagine you have all these things and
are bed-ridden because of ill health? Imagine you have all
these things and good health too, and yet, you have no one
with whom to share them? Or, worse yet you have all of that
and a family, who you never see because of work obligations
to keep your empire running.

For those reasons and more, that is why monetary wealth,
in and of itself, is rarely a viable goal in life. For many, time
is the greatest currency. We can always create more money,
but we cannot create more time. We each are allotted 24
hours in each day. For others wealth may be found in relationships.

Two of the questions I always ask my coaching clients are
"What is it you *really* want?" and "How will you know when
you've got it? About 99.9% of the time the first response is
"money" but as the question sinks deeper into their con-
sciousness, the responses begin to expand. The second
question is frequently a bigger challenge than the first, be-

cause the initial response is rarely accurate. Both questions need time to percolate in order to form a heart-centered response. One that reflects your character and comes from the core of your being.

It turns out, that for most people, it isn't actually about the money; it is what they can do with the money. The elimination of worry is a big one for people, or the ability to help family members and friends. Serving others frequently comes up somewhere between the third and fourth iteration of their response. In a survey at one of our multi-day events, we learned that fully 60% of the respondents had a goal to establish a non-profit charitable organization.

Anytime I read a book on success, self-improvement, or wealth building I consider the author and what it is that qualifies them as an authority on their subject. Did they study the topic and then regurgitate someone else's work? Did they learn the subject, and put their personal spin on what they learned? Or did they study it, learn it, and actually do it? Did they get out there in the trenches, roll up their sleeves, get dirty, take a few hits, and get back on their feet?

As important as these questions are, I also am curious about things like character. Do they have integrity, drive, passion, and a willingness to help others, or are they self-centered quick-buck artists that offer plenty of sizzle and no steak?

When it comes to success literature, there are certain non-negotiables and I'm proud to say that Tim Davis, is a perpetual student who applies his learnings effectively. I've known and worked with Tim for over 10 years and I am honored to call him my friend. We met when he was in one of those valleys of life in which we sometimes find ourselves. It has been amazing to observe him move ever higher from that valley, constantly seeking higher and higher peaks. Even when he takes a hit, and he has taken a few -- he keeps moving forward. Even when he gets knocked back, he gets up, dusts himself off, and keeps going. His attitude, his faith, and his courage are truly inspiring.

He is tenacious in his desire to be the best person he can be. Whether it is being the best husband, boss, dad, friend, or brother in Christ. Tim Davis is a Rock Star, and I am grateful that he took up the challenge to write this book because he is a man whose words are worth reading or hearing.

The idea behind The 5 Steps to Holistic Wealth is a reflection of a journey we can all take, and the best part is that when you have a roadmap, the journey becomes a lot easier. This roadmap comes from real life learning, being, and doing. It comes from a man who knows how to take *effective action* and does so on a daily basis. He is also a guy who knows how to *play full-out* and focus on a goal until it is realized. He doesn't work himself to death, but to **LIFE**!

Tim is a man who has built a collection of assets, businesses, and friends; more than that, he is someone who has created a life that is truly worth living. He continues to develop his mind, his body, and his spirit, and *"The 5 Steps To Holistic Wealth"* can help you do the same!

Let the journey continue...

Augie Byllott

Founder, *Creating Wealth USA*
Founder, *Commonwealth Trust Services*

Why Most Real Estate Inventors are Poor or Have Just Partial Wealth

*During my journey, I battled with many **distractions** and I was able to overcome them. In this book, I will help you to conquer the distractions that have been trying to prevent you from experiencing and sustaining holistic wealth.*

- Why are so many real estate investors stressed?

- Why are so many real estate investors unhealthy and overweight?

- Why are so many real estate investors having unhealthy relationships?

- Why are so many real estate investors struggling financially?

- Why are so many real estate investors not yet able to be generous with their time and money?

The answer to all of the above questions is simple; most real estate investors are still **poor** or have only experienced **partial wealth.**

So many real estate investors focus most of their time and energy to build financial wealth while other areas of their lives are heading towards bankruptcy.

I was an investor who transitioned from poverty, **partial wealth** before experiencing holistic wealth.

At a young age, I set out to prove to my father I was capable of success. I wanted to change the things I was hearing.

I heard the standard things that many kids hear from their parents, "Money doesn't grow on trees", "We are not made of money", "the love of money is the root of all evil", "it is easier for the camel to get through the eye of the needle than for a rich man to get into heaven."

I actually felt that money was scarce, and wealth was elusive. The chances of being wealthy were rare if you weren't born wealthy. Besides, rich people are all crooks and if you become rich, you must have done something wrong. Poverty is more desirable because it is pure and Godlike.

These were the thoughts that were put into my head as a child. When I reached my teenage years, I started having the desire to obtain wealth because my mindset was different. I no longer believed the things I was told as a child.

When I finally tasted the experience of having some money I was hooked. It was like a drug.

I wanted more and more. The sky was the limit. My desire to prove to my father I could succeed became stronger.

However, my mindset of success and wealth became only about money. I was not concerned about any other area of my life. I didn't even think that anything else mattered except money and that was my main focus for many years.

1. TRADING HOURS FOR DOLLARS

At first, I started trading my time for money. I would work hard and as many hours as I possibly could. The more hours I worked the more money I made. In fact, I found that after 40 hours they would pay me 1.5 times what my normal wage was so I would work as many as 70 or 80 hours per week if I could so I could get the big bucks.

Eventually I burned out and everything else in my life began to suffer because of my choice to work so many hours. It wasn't until my world began to fall apart that I realized there was more to life than chasing money. My health was declining. I was not even 30 years old and I had a smokers hack, my kidneys and liver were aching, I was 50 lbs. overweight and my marriage was on the rocks. Not to mention that my support system consisted of a few alcoholic friends that would get with me and commiserate about how bad their lives were too. Life had not turned out like I had expected, and something had to happen.

As I continued in this rat race by working most of my waking hours, not taking care of my body or my family, things started to fall apart. I felt totally out of control and it seemed there was no way to reset. I had money but I had no peace of mind. I had no clarity. My life was in chaos and I was heading towards a complete meltdown.

End It All?

One night my wife at the time came to me and said, "I want a divorce". That made me realize that my world as I knew it was over. There was nothing that I could do at that point to hold it all together. I decided to end it all. I walked down the street to the busy highway, and I was going to walk out into the traffic. As I walked toward my fate, I heard a small voice inside say "STOP." Things can only get better from here.

I had never thought about it until that point, but it dawned on me that **I was the reason for the mess I was in.** I was the one responsible for the situation. If things were going to change, it was up to me to change them. I resolved at that point in my life to change my direction and began to look at everything differently. I decided that I would take the responsibility for what was happening.

At that moment I realized that since I was the one who created the situation, I was the only one who could clean it up. It was up to me to stop my bad habits and create new ones. It was up to me to create the reality that I wanted. No one else was responsible. I couldn't blame anyone.

2. LIFE IS MORE THAN MONEY

I realized right then and there that there was more to life than just money. Deep spiritual thoughts started coming to me. I knew from my Christian upbringing that life was more than just physical. I knew that I needed to go back to my roots and get that spiritual connection. There was a better path than the one that I was on. And it was up to me to find that path, get on it and stay the course.

The importance of my health became a priority. If I did not feel good how could I give my best efforts to the other areas in my life? How could I be my best self at 50 lbs overweight? How could my body give me the 100% energy I needed to keep up with the demands of life when I was abusing my body with harsh and unnatural chemicals? I knew from my upbringing what healthy food looked like. I knew that if you didn't exercise that your muscles would atrophy, and your bones would stiffen up.

I realized how relationships were so very important. I needed to create relationships that lasted making an investment in friends and family so when I needed them, they would be there for me. I recognized that the people that I was hanging around were not helping me but harming me. The toxic relationships were pulling me into them and pulling me down to their level.

Money was still an important part but was no longer my only focus. I realized it was necessary to have but not at the cost of everything else. I had to take a very close look at my perspective on money and see how I could balance my life and money and not let money take control of my life any longer.

And last but not least, I recognized that community needs all of us. We all need to be there giving to others and to be there helping all of our neighbors. Life happens to people every day and it is up to all of us to help in any way that we can.

My Journey

When I realized these five areas were important for me to build holistic wealth, I began searching for the most efficient ways to develop these five areas.

My journey took me into some interesting events. There were a lot of people that had gone before me. There were records of their journeys written in books and if I was going to change my direction then it might be a good idea to read and understand what others had done. I needed to learn how others had overcome their obstacles. My journey took me to places I could not have imagined.

I started with my spiritual life. I knew from my upbringing that there was wisdom in the Bible. So, I began a discipline of reading every day. I needed to know what things to do to get my spirit in order and the Bible was the best place to start. The stories gave good examples of what to do or what not to do. I was able to quickly change my thought patterns. Old habits fell away, and I created new patterns that were conducive with a more balanced life. This was a step in the right direction.

When I quit abusing my body with alcohol and chemicals, I began to notice more energy. I also started making better food choices and walking for exercise and fresh air. Before long I was losing weight. Within a couple of weeks, I had lost 10lbs and was feeling so much better. My mind was becoming clearer and I could focus on so much more. Within 6 months I was a different person. I had to buy all new clothes as everything that I was wearing before was falling off of me. I could now feel good about my appearance and gained self-confidence. The energy that I was feeling was flooding over into all the other areas of my life and my world was changing.

Relationships were a challenge but with my inner peace and my outer changes I was beginning to feel good about developing those relationships that I needed to become a well-rounded individual. It was easier to speak with my children. I was able to find new friends at church and joined some other support groups to get started building those relationships. I enrolled in a night school college and began studying business. That is where I met Sandi my wife. We began our relationship in our 30's and have been married now almost 25 years. I was determined not to screw this up again.

Money, although important, was not the driver that it once was. I realized that there is an abundant supply of everything out there. Scarcity does not even fall into my vocabulary because I see how there is so much. Gratitude for understanding this was something that replaced the greed that used to drive me. I now know that I have everything that I need and that I am wealthy in many more ways than just with money.

Finding a place in the community was a big part of my transformation. Understanding that there are many people that do not know how to receive the abundant resources that are available and are stuck in a mindset that keeps them in poverty.

During my journey, I battled with many **distractions** and I was able to overcome them. In this book, I will help you to conquer the distractions that have been trying to prevent you from experiencing and sustaining holistic wealth.

My journey was challenging because it took me a long time to learn everything, I needed to know to experience holistic wealth. You will not need to invest so many hours and so much money because I have simplified the process for you in this book.

I am passionate to save you time, energy, and money so I will be guiding you through *The 5 Steps To Holistic Wealth* so you can experience or sustain holistic wealth no matter where you are today in your journey.

Let us look at an overview of the 5 steps:

3. THE 5 STEP PROCESS OVERVIEW

In section 2 of this book, I will dive deeper into each step of the holistic wealth process so you can easily build holistic wealth step by step. For now, let us look at an overview of the process so you can understand the simple steps you need to take to build holistic wealth.

THE 5 STEP HOLISTIC WEALTH PROCESS

1. *Spiritual Wealth*

Spiritual Wealth is an abundance of peace that comes from the awareness that you were created to love and live  in the present moment. Anxiety or fear comes from worry about what might happen in the future. Regret comes from what has happened in the past. Living in the now is the only place that we actually have. Having an abundance of this awareness is Spiritual Wealth.

Unfortunately, many real estate investors are currently living their lives regretting their past or worrying about their future. *When you live in the present, you become a present or gift wherever you go.* Good people will be attracted to you because of your magnetic presence.

As we explore the first step to holistic wealth, I will show you why and how to live in the **present** so you can enjoy a wealthy spiritual life.

2. *Physical Wealth*

Physical Wealth is having an abundance of the ability to move and carry out tasks without undue fatigue. Also having the ability to live life fully, with vitality and meaning. It is dynamic and multi-dimensional. Wellness, fitness, health.

At the time of this was written, it is estimated that over 170,000,000 people are either overweight or obese in America. With a population of about 330,000,000 people in America at the time of this publication, that represents a majority of the population. – more than 50%. The estimated medical cost of obesity is over $147 billion. We have become a poor country when it comes to taking care of our physical bodies.

As we explore the second step to holistic wealth, I will show you why and how to build physical wealth so you can live a long and vibrant life.

3. *Relational Wealth*

Relational Wealth is an abundance of valuable, authentic relationships. Created through your interconnections with family, friends, and other human beings.

Many real estate investors currently have some bankrupt relationships because they have neglected to invest quality time to make deposits into their relational wealth.

When we explore the third step to holistic wealth further, I will show you why and how to make deposits into your relational wealth account and avoid bankrupt relationships.

4. *Financial Wealth*

Financial Wealth is an abundance of financial resources that allows a person to have income on a regular basis independent of their daily activities. Financial Wealth also measures the value of all the assets of worth owned by a person offset by any liabilities they might have. Independence from trading hours for dollars.

Many real estate investors are not yet independent from trading hours for dollars.

When we explore the fourth step to holistic wealth further, I will show you why and how you can transition from dependent to independent financial wealth.

5. Community Wealth

Community wealth comes from investing in your local area. You invest by spending time and resources to prop up the groups, families, and individuals that make up your town, city, or affinity group.

I have seen poor communities around our country, and the most common theme that I see is selfishness. The people in the area are only concerned about what is in it for them, and there is no giving back. These communities are poor not for lack of money but for lack of investment from its members. When the members of a community do not give from the wealth of time that they have been given, the area suffers.

When we explore the fifth step to holistic wealth further, I will show you why and how you can invest time and resources to transform your community. Your investment into your community will be a part of your legacy.

SIMPLE HOLISTIC WEALTH ASSESSMENT

Now that the overview is clear, let us begin the journey but before we proceed, we need to understand your current location in your holistic wealth journey. It is time to take the simple holistic wealth assessment.

For each statement below, rank yourself on a scale of 1 to 5, where 1 is unclear and 5 is clear.

STATEMENTS	SCORE
1. I have a simple clear spiritual wealth goal and I invest time consistently to achieve the goal.	
2. I have a simple clear physical wealth goal and I invest time consistently to achieve the goal.	
3. I have a simple clear relational wealth goal and I invest time consistently to achieve the goal.	
4. I have a simple clear financial wealth goal and I invest time consistently to achieve the goal.	
5. I have a simple clear community wealth goal and I invest time consistently to achieve the goal.	
TOTAL	

Add your score and multiply by 4% to determine the percentage score that reflects the current state of your wealth.

For example, if your total score is 15 x 4% = 60% or if your total score is 20 x 4% = 80%.

Score Meaning:

If your score is:

<60%, you currently are living in poverty.

60 – 79%, you have partial wealth.

80 – 100%, you have holistic wealth.

If you currently have poor wealth or poverty, don't be discouraged. I used to have poor wealth before I learned the five steps to holistic wealth. I will show you how to transition so you can experience holistic wealth.

If you currently have partial wealth, you are closer to experiencing holistic wealth. This book will also show you how you can make a few changes consistently so you can experience holistic wealth.

If you currently have holistic wealth, congratulations! This book will show you how to maintain your holistic wealth and take your holistic wealth to the next level.

After you go through the 5 steps to holistic wealth in this book, you can download an assessment template and assess yourself again at ***www.yourholisticwealth.com/score***

Let us now proceed to take the 5 steps and transform your wealth.

The 5 Steps to Holistic Wealth

My life had changed in a
split second, even though my
world had not. I knew there
would still be challenges,
but now I felt confident that
I could meet the challenges
with the faith that I had
in my Creator, and from
that point on, I never
looked back.

STEP 1:
SPIRITUAL WEALTH

1996 was a very dark point in my life. My sixteen-year marriage was on the rocks, and my wife had told me she wanted a divorce. I felt like my life was over because I couldn't see myself without my family. This would change everything. I was embarrassed, humiliated, and ashamed. I had really screwed things up, so I was headed out to put an end to it all. I walked down to a busy road to step out into traffic and let the vehicles seal my fate.

As I walked to my destination, I heard a small voice inside me say, "STOP." And then, "breathe." My next thought was, "things can only get better from here." I began to reflect on my upbringing. My father was an ordained Assembly of God minister, and I was raised in that environment. I knew the difference between what my faith considered right and wrong, and I had chosen to live my life in defiance of how I had been raised.

The conflict between my upbringing and my lifestyle had caused a huge void that I was trying to fill with mind- and body-numbing chemicals that were causing me to spiral out of control. I was about to lose everything. This act of desperation was my attempt to escape from the chaos that this void had created. The reflection into my soul revealed all of this in a single moment, and my mind was completely changed. At that moment, life was new. I had no desire for alcohol or drugs anymore.

My life had changed in a split second, even though my world had not. I knew there would still be challenges, but now I felt confident that I could meet the challenges with the faith that I had in my Creator, and from that point on, I never looked back. Now you might think that everything worked out and everybody lived happily ever after but that isn't what happened. I still ended up getting divorced, fail-ing at a couple of business ventures, going bankrupt, and losing my oldest child to an untimely death. But my faith never wavered after that turning point, no matter what else came my way. It took several months for the divorce to be finalized from my ex-wife telling me she wanted it. I learned a lot during that time and look forward to sharing some of my mistakes with you so you can avoid the pain of making those same mistakes.

Before we proceed, I want to make sure we are on the same page, so there is no confusion or misunderstanding as we talk about spiritual wealth.

What Is Spiritual Wealth?

Spiritual wealth is an abundance of peace that comes from the awareness that you were created to love and live in the present moment. Anxiety and fear come from worrying about what might happen in the future. Regret comes from what has happened in the past. Living in the now is the only place that we actually have peace. Having an abundance of this awareness is spiritual wealth.

Why Spiritual Wealth?

Spiritual wealth is important because the opposite is spiritual poverty. Spiritual wealth enables you to live a holistic life where your spirit, mind and body are integrated as one.

Now that we have a clear definition of spiritual wealth and its importance, let's talk about regret and fear. After my turning point, I had to deal with these two factors, which cause many investors to live in the past or worry about the future instead of living in the present moment with your creator.

Here are some of my regrets:

- I regretted that I didn't make the decision to change my spiritual condition sooner. As a result, I wasted time.

- I regretted that irreparable damage was done to my marriage and family because of my spiritual condition or lack of spiritual deposits, causing broken relationships.

These regrets are real, and I used to dwell on them until I discovered that dwelling on past mistakes is pointless. Instead, I decided to learn from them. I learned that the past is done, and I cannot change it, but I live right now, and I can make better choices now.

Let's look at some fears of the future I used to suffer from:

- I feared not having enough – fear of lack and missed opportunities.

- I feared failing at the things I tried – fear of failure.

- I feared losing what I already had – fear of loss.

These fears caused me to worry about the future until I discovered that I could influence the future by the actions I take today, so I decided to live in the now.

The decision to live in the now or present did not automatically cause my fears to disappear. When my fears reappeared, I took actions that empowered me to overcome them.

The Benefits of Spirit, Mind, and Body Care

The benefits of taking good care of my spirit have been enormous in helping me build spiritual wealth over the years. Making deposits into my spiritual wealth account has given me the connection to God from whom all of creation came. When my spirit is wealthy, the wealth spills over into my mind and my body. My whole being works together and is one.

My mind is at peace because my spirit is connected to God, and my body is healthy. I have no strife or anxiety because I know that everything is going to work out. When my mind is at peace, there is an inexplicable calmness. There is a mind, body, and spirit connection that keeps me in balance, and all the components are working together in unison.

Over the years, I have also discovered that the more I take good care of my body, the quieter my mind becomes, and my spirit connects with God. I have been exercising and eating a better diet for over twenty years now. Part of my turning point experience was to stop putting junk into my body and become focused on getting healthy. I feel younger today than I did back then, and as I have added yoga stretching and weight training, I am stronger in my fifties than I was in my forties.

When I take good care of my spirit, mind, and body, I feel fulfilled. There is no longer a void that is nagging at my insides or an emptiness. There is peace.

How To Build Spiritual Wealth?

To build lasting spiritual wealth, you need to develop a new lifestyle that will enable you to make **consistent** spiritual deposits and withdrawals to keep your spiritual account healthy.

The following activities are highly recommended for spiritual deposits and withdrawals:

Deposits – How to make spiritual deposits.

- Reading the Bible and inspirational material/books
- Prayer and meditation
- Giving and caring for your fellow humans
- Thanksgiving
- Hanging out with people of faith
- Fasting

Withdrawals – How to make necessary withdrawals.

- Asking God for help
- Requesting help from others
- Humbly receiving help from others

The core spiritual deposits and withdrawals are summarized in greater detail below with some recommended consistencies:

- ***Reading the Bible and Inspirational Material***

  This should be a daily inspirational habit. I receive wisdom and understanding from my daily reading.

- ***Prayer and Meditation***

  To build spiritual wealth, a practitioner should pray and meditate daily. Quieting my mind and focusing on my spirit and connection with my Creator is done at 4:15 am every day. Taking that first hour in the morning when I get up helps me start my day on the right foot.

- ***Thanksgiving***

  Thanks should be given on a daily basis. I have created a habit of being thankful when I get into bed and when I get out of bed every day. It is good to develop habits and stack them with things that you do regularly.

- ***Fellowship with others***

  Assembling together should be done consistently. I have a group of men that I get together with weekly. This is something that, when done consistently, will make huge deposits in each group member's life and to your spiritual wealth.

- ***Fasting***

  Fasting and discipline are not only good for your mind and spirit, but they actually allow your physical system to reset. I have fasted for a day, for three days in a row, and for ten days in a row. It is a good idea to do an extended fast at least once or twice a year to really cleanse the mind, body, and spirit, and discipline is very important.

Now that we have covered how to build spiritual wealth, let us now proceed to help you accomplish your spiritual goals.

SPIRITUAL WEALTH GOAL

Spiritual Wealth Goal Step 1:
Your Most Impactful Wealth Goals

To make it easy for you to complete Step 1, here is my example:

My current one most impactful spiritual wealth goal for the next one month is to create a habit of investing 30 minutes a day in spiritual meditation.

Account	Start	Goal	End
1. Spiritual	2/15/21	30 minutes per day.	3/15/21

Your most impactful spiritual goal must have the following three characteristics:

- Your goal must have a **start** and **end** date.
- Your goal must start a **verb** and be **measurable.**
- Your goal must be the most **impactful.**

Here is a specific question to help you to determine your most important goal.

- What is your **ONE** most **impactful** measurable **spiritual wealth** goal for the next one month?

Enter your answers in the template provided below:

Account	Start	Goal	End
1. Spiritual			

Spiritual Wealth Goal Step 2:
Your Most Impactful Daily Activity And Time Budget

Again, to make it easy for you to complete Step 2, here is my example:

My most impactful daily spiritual wealth activity is to start my day with 30 minutes of spiritual meditation.

Activity	Daily Minutes	Week's Total
1. Meditation	30	210

It is now your turn to complete Step 2 of the process so you can identify your most impactful daily spiritual wealth activity and budget time for it.

Your most impactful daily spiritual wealth activity must have the following two characteristics:

- Your spiritual wealth activity must be the most **impactful daily** activity.

- Your spiritual wealth activity's time must be budgeted.

Here is a specific question to help you to identify your most impactful spiritual wealth activity.

- What is your **ONE** most **impactful** daily **spiritual wealth** activity? How many minutes will you budget for this activity?

Enter your answers below:

Activity	Daily Minutes	Week's Total

Spiritual Wealth Goal Step 3:

Schedule Your Most Impactful Daily Activity

Select a time in the day when you cannot easily be distracted and schedule your most impactful activity on your calendar. Here is my example:

Activity	Daily Schedule
1. Meditation	4:15 – 4:45 am

Here is a specific question to help you to determine the most productive time to do your spiritual wealth activity.

- What time of the day will be the most productive for you to do your daily spiritual wealth activity? Don't over think. Select a time and start. You can make necessary changes in the future.

Enter your answers below:

Activity	Daily Schedule

STEP 2:
PHYSICAL WEALTH

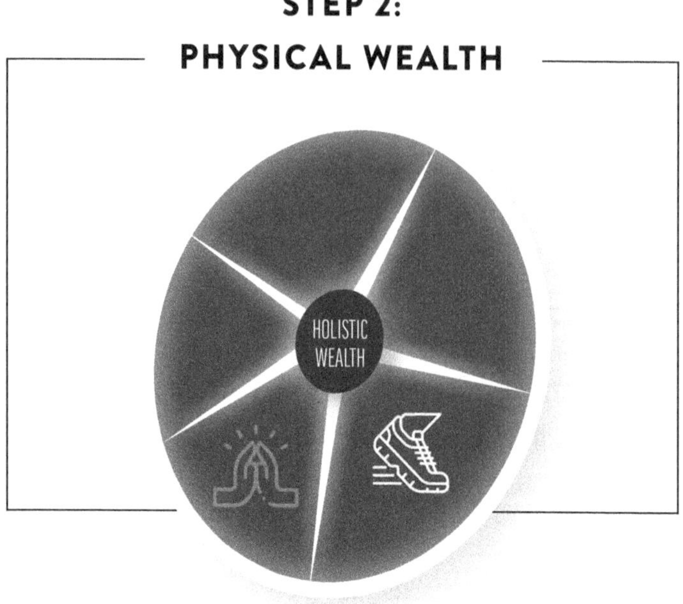

Today in America, it is estimated that over 170 million people are either overweight or obese. If we are a nation of 330 million people, that represents a majority of the population—more than 50%. The estimated medical cost of obesity is over $147 billion. We have become a poor country when it comes to taking care of our physical bodies.

Over 875,000 deaths each year in America are attributed to diseases that are a direct cause of excess weight and obesity (heart disease, stroke, diabetes). This is a problem that needs to be addressed.

Twenty-four years ago. I ignored my body. Because of

the habits that I had created, I was about fifty pounds over-weight, just over the line of being obese. I had a smoker's cough, and I felt a sharp pain in my side, right around my liver. I didn't sleep well, and I felt very sluggish. I was a mess. I had neglected maintenance and repair for my body for many years.

Currently, I feel fantastic. I feel like I am getting younger every year. I am the ideal body weight for my height (based on 106 pounds for the first five feet and then six pounds for each inch above that). I have no pain, and I take no medication. For the last twenty-plus years, I have put a strong emphasis on my physical wealth. That has paid off in so many ways. I sleep soundly and feel good when I wake up. I go to the gym four or five times a week. My immune system is phenomenal; I very rarely get sick. When I do get sick, it is very short-lived.

Living with physical wealth allows you to have a fantastic outlook on your day.

Before we proceed, I want to ensure we are on the same page, so there is no confusion or misunderstanding as we learn how to build physical wealth.

What Is Physical Wealth?

Physical wealth is having an abundance of the ability to move and carry out tasks without undue fatigue. Also, having the ability to live life fully, with vitality and meaning. It is dynamic and multi-dimensional—wellness, fitness, and health.

Why Physical Wealth?

Physical wealth is so important to our wellbeing. A wise teacher said, "If I don't take care of my body, I won't have a place to live." That is very true. Our body is the dwelling place for our spirit. Having a background in construction and residential housing, I know if a house has deferred maintenance and is in poor condition, it becomes very uncomfortable to live in. I have seen houses deteriorate to the point where they are unrepairable and are then slated to be torn down and disposed of.

It is very sad when that happens to a person who is young in age but worn out in body. It doesn't have to be that way. You can live for many years and feel great while you do it.

Here are some of the major benefits of physical wealth:

1. You wake up every morning feeling fresh and rested, ready to meet the demands of your day.

2. You have the energy to play with your children or grandchildren.

3. Your clothes fit, and you feel good about the way you look.

The consequences of physical poverty are:

1. Feeling tired and lethargic most days.

2. Feeling sluggish with no energy to spend time with the important people in your life.

3. Feelings of embarrassment and hopelessness.

How To Build Physical Wealth?

To build lasting physical wealth, you need to develop a new lifestyle that will enable you to make **consistent** physical deposits and withdrawals to keep your physical account healthy.

The following activities are highly recommended for physical deposits and withdrawals:

Deposits – How to make deposits into your physical wealth account.

- Think positive, focus on gratitude.
- Eat a healthy diet
- Exercise and activity
- Sleep well
- Rest and relaxation

Withdrawals – How to make necessary withdrawals

- Extra energy for a difficult task
- Stress from an unforeseen event

- Immune system optimization – ready to defend you when needed.

The core physical deposits and withdrawal principles are summarized in greater detail below with some recommended consistencies:

Physical Wealth Principle #1:
Think Positive with a Focus on Gratitude

Positive thinking has been talked about for a long time. In his book *The Power of Positive Thinking*, Dr. Norman Vincent Peale writes a powerful message of faith and inspiration. Thinking positive with a focus on gratitude sets the stage for good things to come into your life. Nothing happens that doesn't first start in your mind. The first deposit made to a physical wealth account must start with your attitude.

Physical Wealth Principle #2:
Eat a Healthy Diet

I was just saying the other day that I have the best diet plan. I eat whatever I want, whenever I want, and I never gain any weight. The trick is that I have learned to want better foods, smaller portions, and sometimes choose to fast for periods of time. Learning about nutrition is very important if you are going to make this deposit into your account. These days we are confused by so many misleading messages. Unfortunately, many messages are just puffed-up marketing to get you to buy a product. One of the rules I go by is: If it is in a package, you should look closely at it to understand what is really in it. If you can't pronounce the words you see or have no idea what it is, chances are it can make you sick, fat, or both.

Think of the food you eat as fuel for your body, just like an engine. The higher the octane (better quality), the faster and cleaner the engine will fire. If you put better quality fuel in your body, you will get better results. You will have more energy and stamina, and your body will run longer and not wear out as fast.

Physical Wealth Principle # 3:
Exercise and Activity

I cannot stress enough how important exercise and activity are. I had some shoulder pain a while back. My Yoga instructor referred me to a physical therapist to find some exercises to help with the pain. I will never forget the first thing he told me, "Motion is Lotion." In other words, as you move, your joints and muscles actually loosen up. When you keep still, the muscles and joints actually tighten up, and that is what causes pain.

You have probably heard that "sitting is the new smoking." It seems that today, with computers and video games, people are sitting much more than they are moving. This inactivity is causing a big problem. If you want to make some deposits in your physical wealth account, get up and move for five minutes every hour that you are awake. If you make that a consistent habit, it could add years to your life.

Physical Wealth Principle #4:
Sleep Well

People don't typically plan their sleep. We often set alarms for getting up, but we go to bed when we can't stay awake any longer. Then we toss and turn, thinking of what we did and what we have to do until we finally fall asleep, only to wake up three or four times before the alarm goes off. Does that sound like a typical night for you?

Well, it doesn't have to be that way. You can plan your sleep and sleep a lot better when you make some changes. Many of these changes involve your diet, not eating a heavy meal within three hours of bedtime, turning off the screens (tv, computer, phone, etc.) one hour before bed, making your sleeping area dark, getting rid of night lights, and getting a good seven to eight hours of sleep, if that is what your body needs.

Some devices can help you measure the quantity and quality of your sleep. If you want to get serious about your physical wealth account, get serious about your sleep.

Physical Wealth Principle #5:
Rest and Restoration

Everyone needs a little time off. Resting is a law of nature. Rest is the root word for **restoration.** It is so important that God even sets an example of it in the book of Genesis. After he took six days to create the heavens, earth, and all that was in it, he rested on the seventh day. You must unplug. There is no way that you can live your life being on the go seven days a week. That would lead to a breakdown.

I recommend taking at least one day per week and a couple of weeks per year to disconnect from your business and the everyday grind. Plan something that you have never done or just chill out around the house. When this becomes a regular deposit into your physical wealth account, you will be surprised how much more you'll enjoy the time you actually work.

What is the most important thing/goal you do daily, weekly, monthly, quarterly, and yearly to build your physical wealth? Use the table below to enter your answers just like you did with spiritual wealth.

The table below captures a wealthy physical lifestyle system. Now that we have covered how to build physical wealth, let us now proceed to help you accomplish your physical wealth goals.

PHYSICAL WEALTH GOAL

Physical Wealth Goal Step 1:
Your Most Impactful Wealth Goals

To make it easy for you to complete Step 1, here is my example:

My current one most impactful physical wealth goal for the next one month is to eat a healthy diet each day.

Account	Start	Goal	End
2. Physical	2/15/21	Eat healthy meals.	3/15/21

Your most important physical wealth goal must have the following three characteristics:

- Your goal must have a **start** and **end** date.

- Your goal must start a **verb** and be **measurable.**

- Your goal must be the most **impactful.**

Here is a specific question to help you to determine your most important goal.

- What is your **ONE** most **impactful** measurable **physical wealth** goal for the next one month?

Enter your answers in the template provided below:

Account	Start	Goal	End
2. Physical			

Physical Wealth Goal Step 2:
Your Most Impactful Daily Activity And Time Budget

Again, to make it easy for you to complete Step 2, here is my example:

My most impactful daily physical wealth activity is to plan fueling my body for 15 minutes.

Activity	Daily Minutes	Week's Total
2. Plan my meals	15	105

It is now your turn to complete Step 2 of the process so you can identify your most impactful daily physical wealth activity and budget time for it.

Your most impactful daily physical wealth activity must have the following two characteristics:

- Your wealth activity must be the most **impactful daily** activity.

- Your physical wealth activity's time must be budgeted.

Here is a specific question to help you to identify your most impactful physical wealth activity.

- What is your **ONE** most **impactful** daily **physical wealth** activity? How many minutes per day will you budget for this activity?

Enter your answers below:

Activity	Daily Minutes	Week's Total

Physical Wealth Goal Step 3:
Schedule Your Most Impactful Daily Activity

Select a time in the day when you cannot easily be distracted and schedule your most impactful activity on your calendar. Here is my example:

Activity	Daily Schedule
Plan my meals	6:00 - 6:15 am

Here is a specific question to help you to determine the most productive time to do your physical wealth activity.

What time of the day will be the most productive for you to do your daily physical wealth activity? Don't over think. Select a time and start. You can make necessary changes in the future.

Enter your answers below:

Activity	Daily Schedule

STEP 3:
RELATIONAL WEALTH

We were not meant to be alone in our lives. God put us on this planet to thrive and grow, and he put us here with other people to build connections and learn to love. We call this connection a relationship. Relationships, at the very least, can be challenging. They don't happen overnight. Relationships take commitment, compromise, forgiveness, and, most of all, effort. I am by no means a relationship guru, but I have had experience in what deposits need to be made into your relational wealth account and what type of withdrawals can bankrupt you. Believe me, a bankrupt relational wealth account is something you want to avoid.

In my first marriage, things started out great. We were in love and were building on the foundation of a great relationship. We were growing up, having children, and life was good. For the first ten years, I was putting deposits into my relational wealth account with my wife. Then things started to change. The pressure of work and business gave me an excuse to secretly drink alcohol. I needed it to relax and take the edge off. It actually became commonplace for me to begin drinking early in the morning and not stop until I came home—all the while attempting to hide this from my wife and family.

Little by little, I was withdrawing the balance of my relational wealth account. Every day, taking a little more of the credit away and not replacing it with any deposits. Other things that I did also took from the account, and I soon bankrupted my relationship with my wife. It seemed to her the only solution was a divorce. I was relationally bankrupt with no place to go, no reserves at the end of the line.

When you are at the bottom, you can only go up. I was relationally bankrupt, but I knew that there were ways to build good lasting relationships. Not only with a spouse but with everyone that you have a connection with. Whether with a good friend, a business partner, a father, mother, sister, brother, or anyone you might meet, you can build wealth in your relational accounts.

The feeling of satisfaction when there is harmony in your relationships is like no other. As I said above, we are made to connect; we are not made to be alone. Building that account is the focus of this next section, and my goal is to give you some steps you can take to build your relational wealth to abundance beyond your wildest dreams.

Before we proceed, I want to make sure we are on the same page, so there is no confusion or misunderstanding as we talk about relational wealth.

What Is Relational Wealth?

Relational wealth is an abundance of valuable, authentic relationships created through your interconnections with family, friends, and other human beings.

Why Relational Wealth?

Relational wealth is vital in our lives. Building connections with people gives us inner strength, emotional security, and defines our quality of life.

Here are some of the major benefits of relational wealth:

- You gain cooperation from people.
- Your communication is open and honest.
- Your days are filled with satisfaction and harmony.

The consequences of poor relationships are:

- Arguments and fighting

- Distrust

- Distancing and brokenness

How To Build Relational Wealth?

To build lasting relational wealth, you need to develop a new lifestyle that will enable you to make **consistent** relational deposits and withdrawals to keep your relational account healthy.

The following activities are highly recommended for relational deposits and withdrawals:

Deposits – How to make deposits into your relational wealth account.

- Spend time with important people.
- Say thank you.
- Do what you say you're going to do.

Withdrawals – How to make necessary withdrawals.

- Ask for help.
- Depend on others

The core relational deposits and withdrawal principles are summarized in greater detail below with some recommended consistencies:

Relational Wealth Principle # 1:
Respect

As Aretha Franklin taught us in her hit song RESPECT, this is paramount in any relationship. Without it, the relationship dies or becomes adversarial. Respect seems lost in society today as people push their own agendas. How do you show respect in a relationship?

1. Give attention to others.

2. Affirm them and let them know they matter.

3. Be kind, polite, and thankful.

Respect is the first way to make deposits into your relational wealth account.

Relational Wealth Principle # 2:
Active Listening

Actively listening to people you are in a relationship with means fully concentrating on what is being said rather than just passively hearing the words. Active listening requires listening with all your senses. Some examples of active listening are:

1. Paraphrasing what was said to show that you understand.

2. Nonverbal cues to show you understand, such as nodding and eye contact.

3. Leaning forward to engage with the speaker.

Relational Wealth Principle # 3:
Self Awareness

It is useful to reflect, occasionally, on what you are contributing to your relationship. Look in the mirror and ask yourself:

1. Am I judgmental?

2. Am I over critical?

3. Have I treated anyone unfairly or been unkind?

If you find any of this to be true, correct your course, and get back on track to depositing into your relational wealth account. The people in relationship with you will thank you.

Relational Wealth Principle # 4:
Celebrate Each Other

Celebrations happen for birthdays, anniversaries, graduations, and just about any other occasion we choose. Why not celebrate your relationships? Let the people in your life know how much you appreciate them while you still can. Celebrations can look like this:

1. Calling a colleague at work and just tell them how much you appreciate them.

2. Bring your spouse some flowers just to celebrate them.

3. Spend some valuable time with someone you care about and just be present.

Relational Wealth Principle # 5:
Forgive Often

The all-familiar quote, "To err is human; to forgive, divine," puts the act of forgiving someone on a different level. How many times have we needed forgiveness? How many times have we not forgiven someone? Forgiveness makes huge deposits in the relational wealth account.

1. Forgive others when they mistreat you

2. Give love to those who are not loveable.

3. Forgive quickly and often.

Now that we have covered how to build relational wealth, let us now proceed to help you accomplish your relational goals.

RELATIONAL WEALTH GOAL

Relational Wealth Goal Step 1:
Your Most Impactful Relational Goals

To make it easy for you to complete Step 1, here is my example:

My current one most impactful relational wealth goal for the next one month is to send 20 thank you cards.

Account	Start	Goal	End
3. Relational	2/15/21	Send 20 cards	3/15/21

Your most important relational goal must have the following three characteristics:

- Your goal must have a **start** and **end** date.

- Your goal must start with a **verb** and be **measurable.**

- Your goal must be the most **impactful.**

Here is a specific question to help you to determine your most important goal.

- What is your **ONE** most **impactful** measurable **relational wealth** goal for the next one week?

Enter your answers in the template provided below:

Account	Start	Goal	End
3. Relational			

Relational Wealth Goal Step 2:
Your Most Impactful Daily Activity And Time Budget

Again, to make it easy for you to complete Step 2, here is my example:

My most impactful daily relational wealth activity is to write one thank you card each day Monday - Friday. It should take about 5 minutes.

Activity	Daily Minutes	Week's Total
3. Write thank you cards	5	25

It is now your turn to complete Step 2 of the process so you can identify your most impactful daily relational wealth activity and budget time for it.

Your most impactful daily wealth activity must have the following two characteristics:

- Your wealth activity must be the most **impactful daily** activity.

- Your relational wealth activity's time must be budgeted.

Here is a specific question to help you to identify your most impactful spiritual wealth activity.

- What is your **ONE** most **impactful** daily **relational wealth** activity? How many minutes will you budget for this activity?

Enter your answers below:

Activity	Daily Minutes	Week's Total

Relational Wealth Goal Step 3:
Schedule Your Most Impactful Daily Activity

Select a time in the day when you cannot easily be distracted and schedule your most impactful activity on your calendar. Here is my example:

Activity	Daily Schedule
3. Write one thank you card	9:00 - 9:05 am

Here is a specific question to help you to determine the most productive time to do your relational wealth activity.

- What time of the day will be the most productive for you to do your daily spiritual wealth activity? Don't over think. Select a time and start. You can make necessary changes in the future.

Enter your answers below:

Activity	Daily Schedule

STEP 4:
FINANCIAL WEALTH

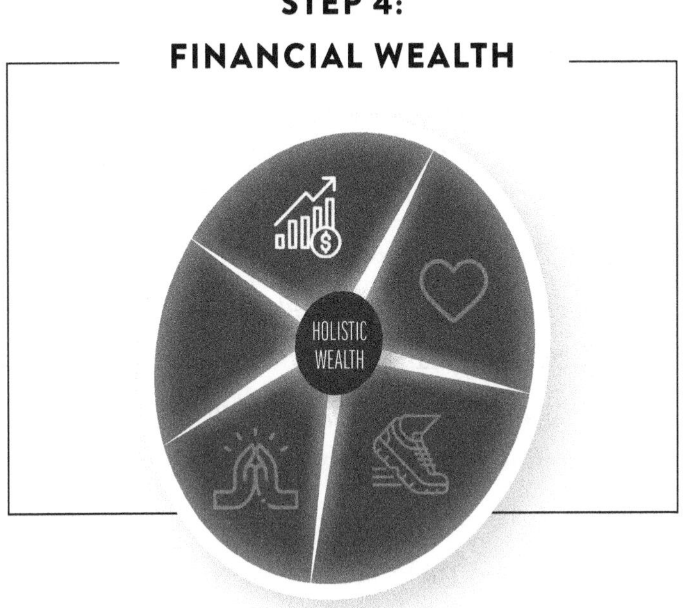

was speaking to a resident of one of our rental properties the other day, and he said, "I am going to be late paying the rent this month because I haven't been getting enough hours at work lately." As I thought about that comment, I realized the mental exercise that individual went through and how he related money he might earn to hours in his day. He was trading his hours for dollars. This type of thinking has been ingrained in our society since before the industrial revolution. Time-based currency exchanges were being experimented with back in the early 1830s. This system has become normal today. Many people measure their worth by how many dollars they are paid each hour.

How does one go from thinking like this, trading hours for dollars, to creating income that comes to you in your sleep? This is the challenge for creating financial wealth. I remember when I first started working, the minimum wage was $3.10 per hour, and gasoline was just over $1.00 per gallon. "Hard work" was something that I was taught to do from an early age, so as I entered the job market, I made an extra effort to earn all that I could. I was earning $5.00 per hour, which was more than the minimum wage, but with a wife and new baby on the way, $200 per week didn't go very far.

I quickly learned that I needed to earn more money. I had a couple of choices. I could work more hours, but I was limited by the 168 hours I had every week. At least thirty percent of that time was spent sleeping. The other option was to find something that could produce income without my time being involved. If such a thing did exist, what did it look like, and where could I find it?

I kind of fell into real estate by accident. My father had purchased a rental property with two units from a real estate investor who was a parishioner at the church my father pastored. It was his first attempt at owning rental real estate. After about a year, he realized that he didn't want to be a landlord, and he offered the property to me. I purchased it and moved into one of the units, and rented the other property out. What really intrigued me was that someone was paying me every month to live in a property next to the house I was living in. That payment came in without me spending my time earning it. From that point on, I was hooked on finding more of that type of income.

Before we proceed, I want to make sure we are on the same page, so there is no confusion or misunderstanding as we talk about financial wealth.

What Is Financial Wealth?

Financial wealth is an abundance of financial resources that allows a person to have income on a regular basis independent of their daily activities. Financial wealth also measures the value of all the assets of worth owned by a person offset by any liabilities they might have—independence from trading hours for dollars.

Why Financial Wealth?

Financial wealth is important because poverty can destroy someone in more ways than one. Poverty can pull the life energy out of people and leave them empty. Poverty can also keep people in a depressed state that can have a lasting effect on their health.

Here are some of the major benefits of financial wealth:

- Financial wealth gives you options for your time.

- Financial wealth allows you to get tools to enhance your life.

- Financial wealth allows you to help others and your community.

Everything that has benefits also has consequences when you refuse to corporate with the principle. The consequences of financial poverty are:

- Lack of resources

- Bondage

- Emptiness

When I started my first business, it was called Tim Davis Home Repair. I was young and naive, thinking that I needed to be the face of my business and do it all. Doing it all was what I did, and it took 70 to 80 hours per week to do it all. Interestingly enough, all I had done was transition from being an employee in a big company to being self-employed and owning a "job." My ego made me think that being self-employed carried some kind of status, but I soon realized that I was fooling myself, which only led to disappointment.

One day as I was working on my truck, I realized that I was in over my head. I was attempting to change an engine, thinking I would be saving money, and it hit me. "There are people that do this for a living, and I could be spending my time doing what I do best if I would only hire them to do this task for me." That epiphany changed my life and set me on the path to creating and working on my business rather than working in my business.

The biggest challenge now was getting past my limiting beliefs that I needed to do everything. Starting the process of building processes and delegating them may seem daunting at first, but doing it will change your life. You will finally build a business that will operate without you being there rather than owning a job that depends on you day in and day out.

It is now time to share with you how to build a business system, so you don't repeat the mistake I made for a long time before my epiphany.

How To Build Financial Wealth?

To build **financial wealth** that provides you with cash flow, using the vehicle of rental real estate, the following simple steps are needed:

Step 1: Define the type of property.

When I began to accumulate rental real estate to build financial wealth, I listed certain criteria that would allow me to know if I would purchase a property. This process made it easy for me to determine if I would move forward with the property purchase.

The first requirement was, I needed to get in with little money out of my pocket because my pockets were remarkably close to empty at the time. This made things a little difficult, but it allowed me to be creative with opportunities that came my way and also allowed me to develop special skills that became valuable as time went on. I had to use techniques such as asking for seller financing or buying properties "subject to" the existing financing (taking over payments).

The second requirement was that after I paid all expenses on the property (which are typically 40% of the rent) and the debt service, I would have at least $100 per month, per door to keep. Cash flow is particularly important as you are building a portfolio. You will be able to increase rents as you study the market and add more management value for the tenants. You should also be able to save money on expenses as you accumulate units into your portfolio, which, in turn, will increase the amount that you will be able to keep, per door, over time.

Step 2: Set a clear goal

When I first began to collect rental properties, I set a clear goal of how many units I would like to accumulate. I developed a spreadsheet and put on the sheet that I would purchase one property per month, and by the end of the year, I would have twelve properties and would be making $1,200 per month net after expenses. I knew at this rate it would take me several years to get to the point where I would have enough passive income for me to survive, but I was willing to put in the consistent work to reach my goal.

The interesting thing about using consistent techniques to find new opportunities is that it works and does so exponentially. As I constantly searched for properties to purchase the first month, I found one. The second month I didn't find any, but the third month I found three. Then again, in month four, I found none. So, although the results were not always reliable, my effort remained consistent.

Then one day, as I searched the market for properties, I came across a tired landlord who wanted to sell thirty units together. I told him I was ready to buy them, but I didn't have any money. We negotiated back and forth, and I purchased all thirty units for no money down. The consistency of searching for property paid off. By the end of the first year, I had accumulated thirty-six rental units, not just the twelve that I set out to acquire. Every month I was now putting $3,600 in my pocket.

Some challenges arose during this time. Negotiating with sellers, dealing with contractors, and finding qualified tenants are some of the challenges that you face. Many sellers feel their property is worth more than it really is. Buying the property at the right price or on the right terms is crucial. When the seller has unreasonable expectations, they are a big challenge to overcome.

Contractors are notorious for not finishing their projects on time and on budget. Coordinating all of the repairs and maintenance can be a huge challenge as you work your way through a project. Keeping this in check will help you overcome this challenge.

Finding qualified tenants is paramount to the success of your rental portfolio. A bad tenant can cost you thousands of dollars and make a good deal turn bad. This is very challenging, but when you do it right, it can give you great cash flow and future profits.

Step 3: Hire a team and transition.

Putting together a team as you build your financial wealth is critical for your success. No one can become financially wealthy on their own. It is a team sport. There is only so much time in a day, and I understood early on that I needed to focus my efforts on the best use of my time. So, putting together a team to help me accomplish my goals was one of the first things I focused on.

Recognizing that it could be challenging to find the right people for my team made me think long and hard about how to accomplish that. The first thing that I did was to look at the person's character. You have to be able to trust your team to always do the right thing. Nothing is more important in the team relationship than trust. The number two trait is competency. They must be competent at what they do. With those two things in place, you will find the right people to be on your team.

The core financial wealth principles are summarized in greater detail below with some recommended consistencies:

Financial Wealth Principle # 1:
Budget Your Money To Control Expenses

Don't spend money you don't have. Budget your money and control your expenses. Ensuring that your outgoings do not exceed your income will take you a long way toward financial wealth. Positive cash flow is essential in investing and important to business in general. Knowing your numbers will help you to not overspend.

Financial Wealth Principle # 2:
Set Income Goals

Set income goals and make plans to reach those goals. You should always have that goal in mind and written out on paper. Refer to it often to see your goals come to fruition. Focus on that number will help you achieve it so much sooner than not having that goal.

Financial Wealth Principle # 3:
Set Aside Money For Investing

Set aside a certain percentage of all of your income to reinvest. Once you start building the portfolio, you will want to allow some of the cash that comes in from it to be reinvested. You will be surprised how quickly it starts to add up and how quickly your portfolio will grow when you intentionally reinvest a percentage of your property. I recommend starting with 10%.

Financial Wealth Principle # 4:
Leverage Your Assets

Leveraging assets is a good way to create more cash flow. Consumer debt is something to stay away from. However, using debt to purchase property can help to create cash flow quicker and more efficiently. Using debt wisely for adding to your portfolio can accelerate you to financial wealth. I recommend that you do not leverage your property more than 75% loan to value. Keeping 25% equity in your property will give you a cushion in the bad times.

Financial Wealth Principle # 5:
Partner Well

If you choose the right people to partner with and the right people on your team, this can also accelerate your financial wealth building. Picking the wrong people or a bad partnership can be devastating and can cause financial failure. I have done both, and believe me choosing the right people to work with is critical. Always consider character and competency when you are considering bringing people on to your team. This will go a long way in your relationships.

Now that we have covered how to build financial wealth, let us now proceed to help you accomplish your spiritual goals.

FINANCIAL WEALTH GOAL

Financial Wealth Goal Step 1:
Your Most Impactful Wealth Goal

To make it easy for you to complete Step 1, here is my example:

My current one most impactful financial wealth goal for the next one month is to make $30,000 net cash flow.

Account	Start	Goal	End
4. Financial	2/15/21	Make $30,000	3/15/21

Your most important financial goal must have the following three characteristics:

- Your goal must have a **start** and **end** date.
- Your goal must start a **verb** and be **measurable.**
- Your goal must be the most **impactful.**

Here is a specific question to help you to determine your most important goal.

- What is your **ONE** most **impactful** measurable **financial wealth** goal for the next one month?

Enter your answers in the template provided below:

Account	Start	Goal	End
4. Financial			

Financial Wealth Goal Step 2:
Your Most Impactful Daily Activity And Time Budget

Again, to make it easy for you to complete Step 2, here is my example:

My most impactful daily financial wealth activity is to meet with team leaders for 60 minutes a day Monday – Friday.

Activity	Daily Minutes	Week's Total
4. Have meetings with team leaders	60	300

It is now your turn to complete Step 2 of the process so you can identify your most impactful daily financial wealth activity and budget time for it.

- Your most impactful daily wealth activity must have the following two characteristics:

- Your financial wealth activity must be the most **impactful daily** activity.

- Your financial wealth activity's time must be budgeted.

Here is a specific question to help you to identify your most impactful financial wealth activity.

- What is your **ONE** most **impactful** daily **financial wealth** activity? How many minutes will you budget for this activity?

Enter your answers below:

Activity	Daily Minutes	Week's Total

Financial Wealth Goal Step 3:
Schedule Your Most Impactful Daily Activity

Select a time in the day when you cannot easily be distracted and schedule your most impactful activity on your calendar. Here is my example:

Activity	Daily Schedule
4. Meet with team leaders	2:00 - 3:00 pm

Here is a specific question to help you to determine the most productive time to do your financial wealth activity.

What time of the day will be the most productive for you to do your daily financial wealth activity? Don't over think. Select a time and start. You can make necessary changes in the future.

Enter your answers below:

Activity	Daily Schedule

STEP 5:
COMMUNITY WEALTH

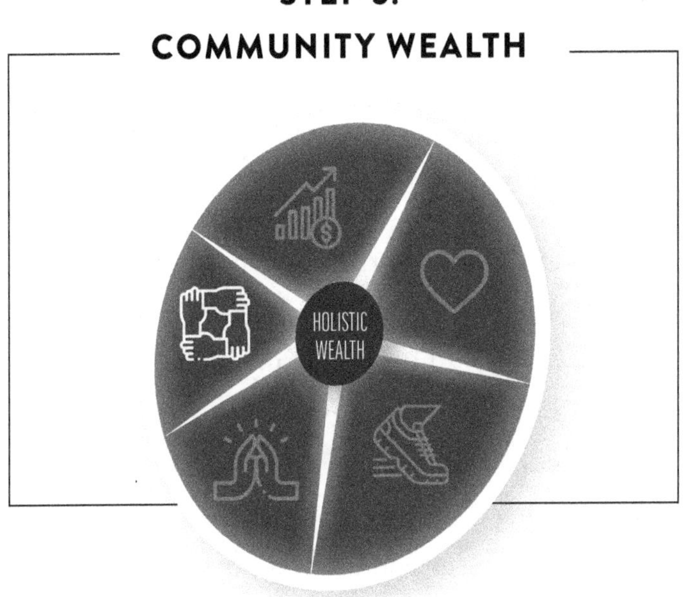

Community wealth starts with involvement. Is there a group of people that you have a special connection with? Maybe a particular religious group, service club, community center, or charitable organization? We are not islands. We were designed to connect with other humans and giving back through community involvement creates community wealth.

I have seen poor communities around our country, and the most common theme that I see is selfishness. The people in the area are only concerned about what is in it for them, and there is no giving back. These communities are poor not for lack of money but for lack of investment from its members. When the members of a community do not give from the wealth of time that they have been given, the area suffers.

I remember a time in my life when I was living in community poverty. I took no time for my community. I spent no time in church or gathering together. I did not reach out to charity groups. I did not help my fellow humans. This was the dark time in my life where I was consumed with myself. When I finally realized that there was a better way, I found that being a part of the community and investing in it not only changed the community, but it changed me.

I found a different perspective. I found love for my fellow humans. I found the energy that I received from being connected and being a part of something bigger than myself. I found community wealth.

One of the programs that I have been involved in is called Paint Your Heart Out. This program was designed to find people in our community that owned their own house but could not maintain it, perhaps because of age or illness. The leaders of this organization would identify a family in need and then organize a day when volunteers would come out and would repair and paint the exterior of the recipients' house.

One of these houses belonged to a nice older lady whose story was heartbreaking. A year prior to the time we were going to paint, her husband was getting ready to do the work when he had a massive heart attack and died. She did have children; however, they lived out of state and were not financially able to move back to Florida when this all happened.

Our group was assigned to take care of this particular house. Since I had construction experience, I volunteered to do a pre-inspection of the house so we could be better prepared to get the project done. When I met with her, she told me the story, and it was so satisfying when we completed the project to see the huge smile on her face.

Before we proceed, I want to make sure we are on the same page, so there is no confusion or misunderstanding as we talk about community wealth.

What Is Community Wealth?

Community wealth comes from investing in your local area. You invest by spending time and resources to prop up the groups, families, and individuals that make up your town, city, or affinity group.

Why Community Wealth?

Community wealth building is crucial to your welfare and that of your surrounding area. Poverty comes in like a thief to steal your serenity. Community wealth will stand as a deterrent to poverty. Investing in a community helps you to experience meaning and fulfillment.

Here are some of the significant benefits of community wealth:

- Happy neighbors

- Safe neighborhoods

- Good jobs

Here are some of the consequences of community poverty:

- Crime

- Hunger

- Decay

How To Build Community Wealth?

To build lasting community wealth, you need to develop a new lifestyle that will enable you to make **consistent** community deposits and withdrawals to keep your community wealth account healthy.

The following activities are highly recommended for community deposits and withdrawals:

Deposits

- Invest time and resources to help with community projects.

- Join civic groups that offer economical and volunteer help.

- Support your local first responders and help them when they need your assistance.

Withdrawals

- When you see a need in your community, ask others to help with that need.

- Helping others and working together will make you feel better.

- Giving back to your community also creates a reputation and gives you credibility.

The core community wealth principles are summarized in greater detail below with some recommended consistencies:

Community Wealth Principle # 1:
Your Community Reflects On You

The person you look at in the mirror every morning will show up in your community. Your community is going to look like that person. The attitude you show up with to the things you do will be evident as you interact with those around you.

Community Wealth Principle # 2:
You Reflect Your Community.

Just as you show up in your community, your community will show up in you. This is a principle that is true no matter what environment you are in. People typically become a product of their environment.

Community Wealth Principle # 3:
It Takes a Village

Community wealth building is a team effort. You cannot do this on your own. You must incorporate the help and effort of others to get the results of community wealth.

Community Wealth Principle # 4:
Make a Commitment and be Consistent.

Making a commitment to a group or an organization is important. Being consistent with your commitment is even more important.

Community Wealth Principle # 5:
Say a Prayer for your Community.

Prayer changes things, so asking God to help your community is something that will make a difference. I say a short prayer daily and ask that my community be blessed and for God to protect the leaders and those who serve.

Now that we have covered how to build community wealth, let us now proceed to help you accomplish your community goal.

COMMUNITY WEALTH GOAL

Community Wealth Goal Step 1:
Your Most Impactful Wealth Goal

To make it easy for you to complete Step 1, here is my example:

My current one most impactful community wealth goal for the next one month is to complete 1 charitable project.

Account	Start	Goal	End
5. Community	2/15/21	Complete 1 charitable project	3/15/21

Your most important community goal must have the following three characteristics:

- Your goal must have a **start** and **end** date.

- Your goal must start a **verb** and be **measurable.**

- Your goal must be the most **impactful.**

Here is a specific question to help you to determine your most important goal.

- What is your **ONE** most **impactful** measurable **community wealth** goal for the next one month?

Enter your answers in the template provided below:

Account	Start	Goal	End
5. Community			

Community Wealth Goal Step 2:
Your Most Impactful Daily Activity And Time Budget

Again, to make it easy for you to complete Step 2, here is my example:

My most impactful daily spiritual wealth activity is to read my Bible for 20 minutes per day Monday – Sunday.

Activity	Daily Minutes	Week's Total
5. Plan	20	140

It is now your turn to complete Step 2 of the process so you can identify your most impactful daily community wealth activity and budget time for it.

Your most impactful daily wealth activity must have the following two characteristics:

- Your wealth activity must be the most **impactful daily** activity.

- Your community wealth activity's time must be budgeted.

Here is a specific question to help you to identify your most impactful spiritual wealth activity.

- What is your **ONE** most **impactful** daily **community wealth** activity? How many minutes will you budget for this activity?

Enter your answers below:

Activity	Daily Minutes	Week's Total

Community Wealth Goal Step 3:
Schedule Your Most Impactful Daily Activity

Select a time in the day when you cannot easily be distracted and schedule your most impactful activity on your calendar. Here is my example:

Activity	Daily Schedule
5. Plan	7:30 – 7:50 am

Here is a specific question to help you to determine the most productive time to do your community wealth activity.

- What time of the day will be the most productive for you to do your daily community wealth activity? Don't over think. Select a time and start. You can make necessary changes in the future.

Enter your answers below:

Activity	Daily Schedule

Pulling It All Together

The American Society of Training and Development studied accountability and found you have a 65% chance of completing a goal if you commit to someone. But you can increase that likelihood of success to 95% if you have an 'accountability appointment' with the person you committed to.

ONGRATULATIONS! NOW THAT YOU HAVE SET clear holistic wealth goals for each wealth account, let us put your goals, number of minutes you will invest each day and the time of the day into three summary templates.

As usual, I will lead with my example.

My Most Important Holistic Wealth Goals Summary

Account	Start	Goal	End
1. Spiritual	2/15/21	Meditate 30 minutes per day.	3/15/21
2. Physical	2/15/21	Eat healthy meals.	3/15/21
3. Relational	2/15/21	Send 20 cards	3/15/21
4. Financial	2/15/21	Make $30,000	3/15/21
5. Community	2/15/21	Complete 1 charitable project	3/15/21

Now, it is your turn. Summarize your most important holistic wealth goals for the next one month. Just pull the information from the goals section at the end of each holistic wealth step above and summarize the goals here with the appropriate dates.

Your Most Important Holistic Wealth Goals Summary

Account	Start	Goal	End
1. Spiritual			
2. Physical			
3. Relational			
4. Financial			
5. Community			

My Most Impactful Daily Actions And Minutes

Activity	Daily Minutes	Week's Total
1. Meditation	30	210
2. Plan my meals	15	105
3. Write thank you cards	5	25
4. Meeting with team leaders	60	300
5. Plan charitable activity	20	140
Total	**130**	**780**

From my summary table above, I just need to invest 130 minutes or 2.16 hours a day and 780 minutes or 13 hours a week to build holistic wealth.

That is just about 9% (130/1440) of my day or about 8% (780/10,080) of my week to build holistic wealth. Building holistic wealth is not complicated. It just requires the consistent investment of time.

Now, it is your turn. Summarize your most impactful daily actions and minutes. Just pull the information from the goals section at the end of each holistic wealth step above and summarize the actions and minutes below:

Your Most Impactful Daily Actions And Minutes

Activity	Daily Minutes	Week's Total
Total		

What percentage of your day do you need to invest to build holistic wealth?

Simply divide your total daily minutes by 1440 minutes which is the total number of minutes per day. For example, if your daily total is 150 minutes, then you are investing 150/1440 = 10%.

What percentage of your week do you need to invest to build holistic wealth?

Simply divide your total weekly minutes by 10,080 minutes which is the total number of minutes per week. For example, if your daily total is 875 minutes, then you are investing 875/10,080 = 9%.

My Most Impactful Daily Schedule

Activity	Daily Schedule
1. Meditation	4:15 – 4:45 am
2. Plan my meals	6:00 – 6:15 am
3. Write thank you cards	9:00 am – 9:05 am
4. Meet with team leaders	2:00 – 3:00 pm
5. Plan charitable event	7:30 – 7:50 am

I consider the above schedule as my distraction free schedule. I fight to protect this schedule because I am determined to build and maintain holistic wealth.

Now, it is your turn. Summarize your most impactful daily schedule. Again, just pull the information from the goals section at the end of each holistic wealth step above and summarize the schedule below:

Your Most Impactful Daily Schedule

Activity	Daily Schedule

Protect your schedule and refuse to allow **distractions** to prevent you from building and sustaining holistic wealth.

You can download weekly planning templates at: *www.yourholisticwealth.com/plan*

Now that you have clear holistic wealth goals, impactful daily actions and an impactful daily schedule, there is one more habit that will enable you to build and sustain holistic wealth. The habit is; **accountability.**

CONSISTENT ACCOUNTABILITY

The American Society of Training and Development (ASTD) studied accountability and found you have a 65% chance of completing a goal if you commit to someone. But you can increase that likelihood of success to 95% if you have an 'accountability appointment' with the person you committed to.

We strongly recommend you establish two levels of accountability:

Personal Accountability

Personal accountability should be done daily and weekly, focusing on your consistency rate. Your consistency rate drives the achievement of your most important wealth goals.

What time will you hold yourself accountable each day for your results? For example, I hold myself accountable daily at 5:00 – 5:15 am for the previous day. I go over my calendar from the previous day and make sure that I accomplished what I set out to do. Then I make sure that my schedule for the upcoming day is planned out.

Schedule your accountability time on your calendar and be serious to invest that time to hold yourself accountable each day.

Community Accountability

Community accountability should be done weekly, monthly, quarterly, and yearly, focusing on your consistency rate and monthly, quarterly, and yearly wealth results scoreboards.

I review with my assistant what the previous weeks achievements where during our Monday morning meeting. This activity is also done monthly and quarterly. At the end of each year there is one day set aside with my team to review our accomplishments for the year and make sure we have clear goals for the upcoming year.

Find or form an accountability team within your business and outside of your business. These teams will help to hold you accountable weekly, monthly, quarterly, and yearly so you can achieve your most important holistic wealth goals faster. When will you schedule the time for your community accountability?

CONSISTENT HOLISTIC WEALTH BUILDING

To build and sustain holistic wealth, do the following consistently:

1. *Daily:*

- Invest time to do the wealth building activities on your daily schedule.

- Evaluate your day each day so you do not get off track.

2. *Weekly:*

- Plan your week using the weekly planning template which you can download for free at ***www.yourholisticwealth.com/plan***

3. *Monthly:*

- Track your results on a monthly scoreboard.

There are weekly, monthly, quarterly, and yearly scoreboards in our ***Wealth to More Wealth Workbook.*** A scoreboard enables you to see how you are doing and adjust your game plan when necessary.

Order a copy at
www.yourholisticwealth.com/workbook

ABOUT THE AUTHOR

Tim Davis is an entrepreneur that dreams big and has a driving purpose to add value to people's lives. With over 40 years of experience in real estate, Tim enjoys sharing the wealth of knowledge and skills that he has developed with others, so they can build holistic wealth.

As an active investor and business owner, he continues to learn and grow his skill set to meet the current market. He has a large portfolio of rental properties and his real estate offices, which manage over 500 units, focus on helping real estate investors maximize the return on their investments and build wealth.

A great source of inspiration for Tim is that of Andrew Carnegie—he built a hugely successful company, and towards the end of his life, he donated the majority of his fortune and wealth to make the world a better place. Although Andrew Carnegie died over 100 years ago, you can still find the Carnegie Foundation for the Advancement of Teaching is still going strong investing in education all over the United States.

Tim is passionate about adding value to people's lives and looks forward to adding value to your life so you can grow your current wealth to the next level holistically. To get more wealth building value, go to ***www.yourholisticwealth.com***

ACKNOWLEDGMENTS

We are all becoming something more than we were the day before. Our lives are a journey of ups and downs and we meet people along the way who inspire us to be all we can. I have met many such people along the way. Some of them I met through books and some in person.

One of those that I read about was Joseph the son of Israel. He had a lot of adversity in his life. His brothers sold him as a slave. He ended up in a place of authority and was wrongfully accused. He ended up in prison and then was exalted to second in command for the whole country of Egypt. I am sure that during the rough times that he felt discouraged but there was probably a glimmer of hope inside that he would be able to overcome the adversity. He never gave up and it ended well for him. That is the spirit of someone who believes. When they have that faith, they know that things will get better and they do.

Our bodies are amazing. They are resilient and give us a very comfortable place to live as long as we take care of them and don't abuse them. An inspiration in Physical Wealth has been my Yoga instructor Marni Tamayo from Yoga Point in Lakeland Florida. When I first met with her I told her that I wanted to be more flexible. I had become very stiff from constantly sitting in front of a computer at my work. She patiently showed me how to move, stretch and hold those poses so that I could accomplish that goal. Every day I hold some of the poses that she taught me and I think of how much better shape I am in because of what I learned.

Also, Ellen Latham the creator of Orange Theory Fitness created the perfect workout program for me. The way that they have structured classes with coaches to keep you accountable to do what you are supposed to do to get your heart rate up and push your muscles, has kept me focused on working out. To date I have actually attended over 900 one-hour classes and it has really changed my life.

Relationships can be hard, but my wife Sandi has taught me that accepting each other with all the little quirks that each of us have is the only way that we can make it. I really appreciate that about her, and she has been an inspiration for me in so many ways. This year we celebrate 24 years of marriage. She has allowed me to be and do what I want and that has been a huge catalyst for me to become what I have become. It has been said behind every good man is a good woman and I know that to be true.

Also, my ex-wife Wanda, had it not been for the turning point in my life that happened because of the decision made to divorce, I would not have had the wakeup call that I had and would have probably stayed on a path that would have eventually ended badly for me. Even though that was a very hard time for me I learned so much and looking back I am grateful. We have to this day remained cordial and I hold no grudge and have no ill feelings towards her.

Many people credit Napoleon Hill's "Think and Grow Rich" book as one that got them to thinking. I actually looked into it a little deeper and asked who was this Andrew Carnegie that caused Napoleon to spend 20 years of his life writing a book. What I found when I studied Andrew Carnegie's life was that of an entrepreneur who was a phenomenal "people picker". He knew more about the psychology of human beings than most of his era. I loved the fact that Mr. Carnegie, though he became the richest man of his time, was a good steward of his resources and gave back to the world the Financial Wealth that he accumulated. That is an inspiration for us all.

Our world seems divided when you look at it from a 30,000-foot view but it is inspiring when you see people that bring us together for a common purpose. Such is that of the Rotary International. I have been a part of that organization for many years. Rotary set out years ago to eradicate the world of the dreaded disease of Polio. Through the Rotary Foundation and Rotary Clubs all over the world they have almost accomplished that goal. They also help in local communities and that is why I believe in what they do. I will always be a supporter of Rotary International.